· CLOTHING ·

Underwear

Helen Whitty
POWERHOUSE MUSEUM

This edition first published in 2002 in the United States of America by Chelsea House Publishers, a subsidiary of Haights Cross Communications.

Chelsea House Publishers
1974 Sproul Road, Suite 400
Broomall, PA 19008-0914

The Chelsea House world wide web address is www.chelseahouse.com

Library of Congress Cataloging-in-Publication Data Applied for.

ISBN 0-7910-6575-8

First published in 2000 by
Macmillan Education Australia Pty Ltd
627 Chapel Street, South Yarra, Australia, 3141

Copyright © Powerhouse Museum, Sydney 2000

Unless otherwise indicated, all objects featured in this publication are from the Powerhouse Museum collection. The Museum acknowledges the many generous donations of objects which form a significant part of its collection.

Please visit the Powerhouse Museum at www.phm.gov.au

Curatorial advice: Lindie Ward, Glynis Jones, Claire Roberts and Christina Sumner of the Powerhouse Museum
Photography: Powerhouse Museum including Penelope Clay, Marinco Kojdanovski, Sue Stafford and Nitsa Yioupros (unless indicated in the picture acknowledgement)
Photo librarian: Kathleen Hackett
Research librarian: Ingrid Mason
Rights and permission officers: Gara Baldwin and Judith Matheson
Editorial and production assistance: Judith Matheson
Other assistance: Stephanie Boast, Fleur Bishop, Suzanne Chee, Mandy Crook, Heleanor Feltham and Joan Watson
Powerhouse Publishing Manager: Julie Donaldson

Edited by Michaela Forster, em rules pty ltd
Text design and page layout by Polar Design Pty Ltd
Cover design by Polar Design Pty Ltd
Illustrations by Wendy Arthur

Printed in Hong Kong

Contents

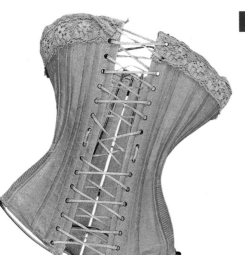

Don't turn this page!
Think of what you wear right next to your skin during the day and at night—your underwear and sleepwear. See if you recognize some of the underwear and sleepwear in this book. There are some strange and wonderful ways of dressing!

Introduction

The things you wear on your body are your clothes. You probably have things you like to wear and things you have to wear. Your family probably likes you to wear special clothes for certain occasions. Sometimes what you like to wear and what your family wants you to wear are very different. Have you heard someone say, 'I wouldn't be caught dead in that dress/jacket/hat/shoes'? People can feel very strongly about what they, and others, wear.

The story of clothing is about people's creativity and the ways they like to show it. What people make, wear and care about are examples of this creativity. What people wear says something about them. *Clothing* looks at wearing and making clothes across times, places and cultures.

Don't get dressed up to read this book —just dust off your imagination. Start off by imagining yourself without clothes.

Too revealing? The strange thing is, the more you cover up with clothing, the more you are really saying about yourself.

▼ 'FUNK INC' poster from funkessentials, designed and made in Australia, 1993

FUNK inc

funkessentials

You're ugly and your mother dresses you funny

▶
Transparent plastic figure of a woman. It is full size, and shows the body organs, veins and arteries. It was made in 1954 to teach people about health and hygiene.

Underclothes: the secret clothes

This book looks at the history of the clothes we hide from other people—what we wear to bed, in the house at night or when we are sick.

It looks at underwear that was once outerclothes, and outerclothes that were once underwear. For hundreds of years, a shirt was thought of as men's underwear as it was often hidden beneath a jacket.

Sometimes the names for men's underwear become the names for women's underwear, and the other way around. *Pantaloons à pont*, similar to what sailors wear, are pants that open at the front like a bridge (*pont* is the French word for 'bridge'). *Pantaloons* became 'pants' for men but 'panties' for women.

◀ A **linen** or cambric woodsman's smock made by hand in England. The style of the shirt suggests it was underwear, but the thick fabric says outerwear.

▶ A nightdress and brunch coat ensemble made of nylon by Texwear, Australia, around 1965.

◀ A yellow evening dress made in the 1950s. The bodice is lined with bone to make it stiff.

To protect the body from the cold

One of the reasons we wear underwear is to keep warm. For example, in the early 1850s, women began to wear bright-colored quilted petticoats in cold weather. Red woollen fabric called **flannel** was very popular. Around this time, flannel was used all over Europe for men's winter underwear, which became known as 'red flannels'.

▼ This mannequin is wearing 'combinations'. They combine a woollen vest with pants for either a man or woman to wear. Combinations were also made of linen and cotton.

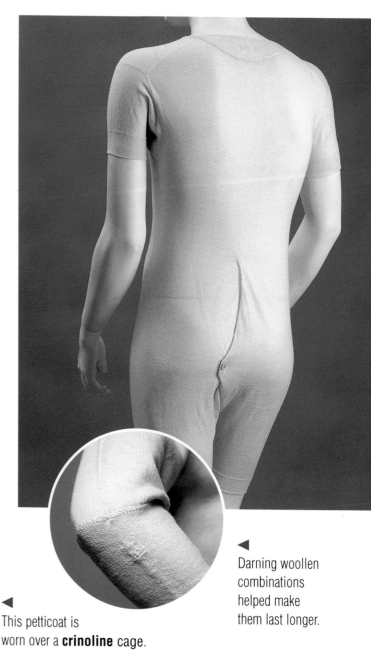

◄ This petticoat is worn over a **crinoline** cage.

◄ Darning woollen combinations helped make them last longer.

To support the shape of outerclothes

Body shapes change with fashions. What people wear underneath their clothes is a big part of what their outerclothes will look like—even if they do not wear underwear at all! Women seem to have changed shape dramatically over the centuries—more so than men. Underwear such as petticoats, bras, slips, **corsets**, **bustles** and crinolines were all used to change the shape of outerclothes.

Imagine what the models below are wearing beneath their dresses. One is wearing complicated underwear, the other may be wearing little underwear at all!

► In the 1870s, the fashion was to look like you had a big bottom. Women and girls wore a bustle under their clothes to make the right shape.

◄ This gold rayon evening dress was made in Australia by Lucy Secours between 1935 and 1945. It is likely that to achieve the long sleek look of this dress, slinky, silken panties, camiknickers or camibockers would have been worn.

◄ This silk open robe dress was made in the 1760s. **Panniers** gave this dress and the woman wearing it the fashionable shape in Europe in the 1700s. Panniers (also called baskets) were false wide hips.

To alter the shape of the body

Berlei is a company that makes underwear. In the 1920s, it made and sold underwear based on research. People who sold the underwear measured 6,000 women on Sydney beaches and in factories. Berlei analyzed all the measurements, and decided that there were five figure types. Berlei started to advertise that the correct underwear could improve women's posture— the way they stand or hold their bodies.

▼ Berlei advertisements showing how its underwear could change women's shape and posture, 1930s.

BERLEI - CAMP SUPPORT 117

BERLEI SCIENTIFIC RESEARCH
reveals
Five Australian Figure Types
Berlei

Stand up and Live

THE BERLEI WAY to beauty

To keep other clothes clean

Q What are these?
(Hint: Look at the photographs of Julia on pages 16 and 17.)

The answer is on page 30.

> *In the beginning of the present century, it was thought proper for a gentleman to change his undergarments three times a day.*
>
> From *The Habits of Good Society*,
> J. Hogg & Sons, London, 1855

Go back to England 300 years ago and one thing that may surprise you is the smell! Wealthy people's underwear was perfumed to disguise the smell of dirty bodies. Underwear kept the skin away from the outerclothes. Outerclothes were usually made from expensive fabrics that were difficult to wash. Underwear was made of fabrics that were easier to wash.

In the 1600s, some people believed that bathing was unhealthy, and even wrong. However, Queen Elizabeth I took a bath once a month 'whether she needed it or not.' Some religions and cultures believed in bathing, while others did not.

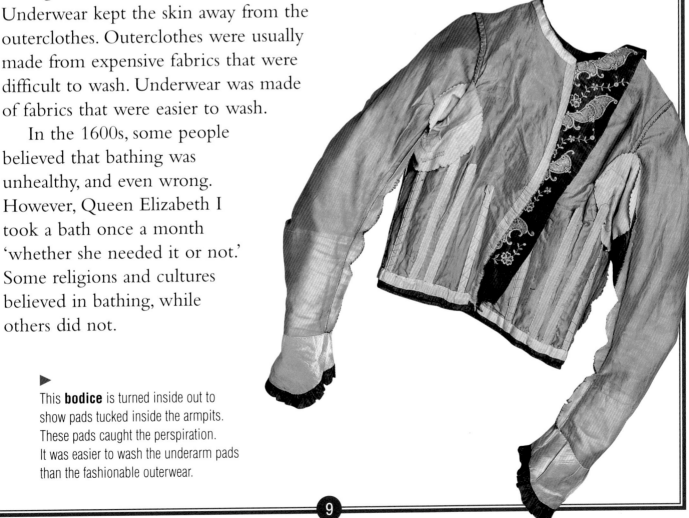

► This **bodice** is turned inside out to show pads tucked inside the armpits. These pads caught the perspiration. It was easier to wash the underarm pads than the fashionable outerwear.

To please the wearer

Underwear are secret garments. With secrets you are careful about who you tell. With underwear you are careful about who you show. Very few people see your underwear or what it covers. Sometimes only you do!

In the 1700s, European women no longer wore layers and layers of petticoats to give them the fashionable shape. They wore a petticoat with cane hoops sewn into it. Ladies would have a bell shape from the waist down. Their legs and ankles were hidden except when they walked and their hoops would swing from side to side. Far from keeping it a secret, their underwear almost made a display!

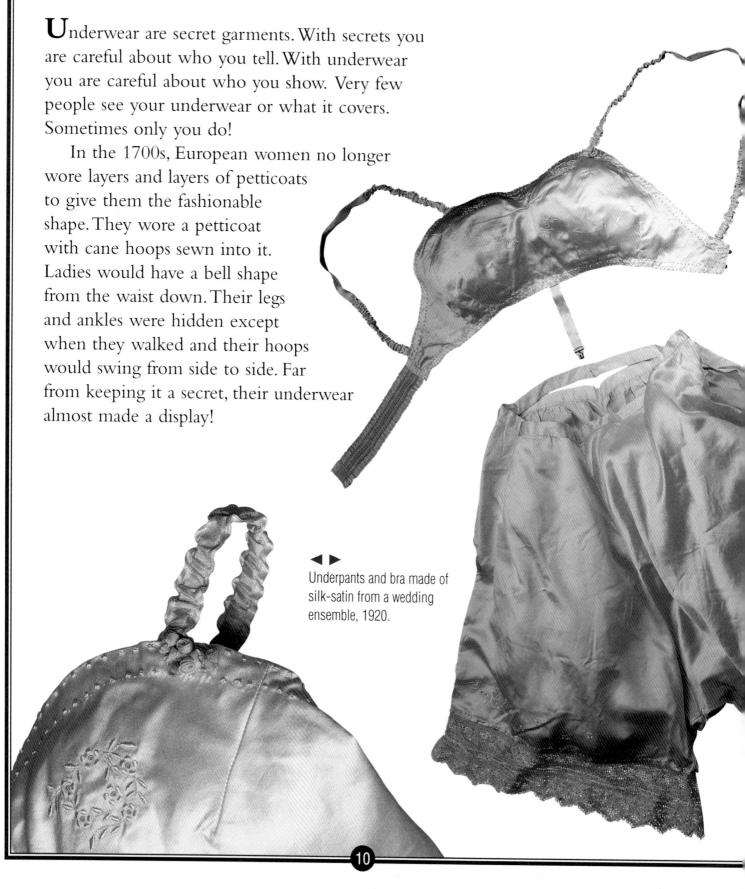

◄ ►
Underpants and bra made of silk-satin from a wedding ensemble, 1920.

▲ A body stocking made of black net, designed by Giorgio Armani, Italy, 1994–95.

▼ Daisy bra and pants made of nylon by Berlei, Australia, 1970.

► A women's **camisole** made of cotton by Berlei, 1925.

What they were wearing then

Ada Lovelace was born in 1815 in England. When she was 21 years old, she began working with Charles Babbage on his 'analytical engine'— an early computer. Ada thought of the idea of computer programming using cards.

Ada is likely to have worn these undergarments:
- a knee-length shift called a **chemise**
- cotton open-**drawers** tucked and trimmed with lace
- a petticoat with embroidery around the bottom and rows of **piping** at the knee
- a tightly laced corset, as a small waist was the fashion of the day
- a bustle.

Ada Lovelace

Bustles

It has been fashionable over the centuries for women to have a big bottom! Fashionable ladies in medieval times padded their clothes around their bottom. In the 1600s, some women wore a thick bolster, commonly called a bum-roll, under their skirts. One hundred years later, this 'false rump' was stuffed with cork or cushion stuffing. Sometimes a bustle was made with horsehair. In the late 1800s, bustles were made with rows of whalebone or cane placed from the sides around the back.

▼ This bustle, worn over a petticoat, is tied around the waist and hips.

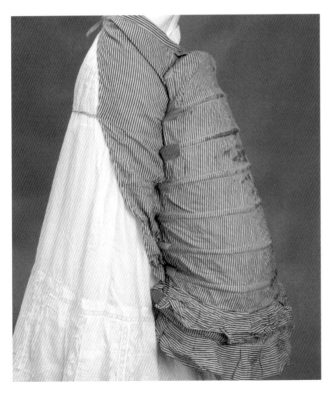

▲ This bustle is made of nylon. It is a copy of bustles made from horsehair braid.

Corsets

Corsets are like a wide belt around your middle. They reduce the size of your waist. Corsets were worn by men, women, girls and boys for hundreds of years. Advertisements for men's corsets were still seen in 1920.

Boys and girls were dressed as miniature grown-ups until the late 1800s. Little corsets (also called 'staybands'), were put on babies. From the age of ten years, girls wore a bodice.

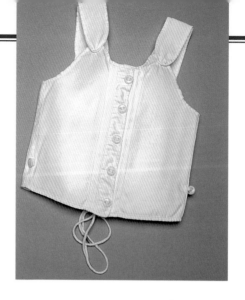

◄ A baby's corset

► This corset was made in England between 1860 and 1870.

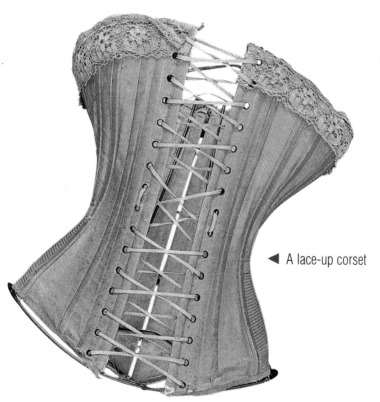

◄ A lace-up corset

► This corset was made in the 1750s. The material has worn away and we can see how it was made. The sticks of whalebone were sewn into the corset to make it stiff and keep the body firm. It has layers of fabric stitched together by hand.

Petticoats

The petticoat was a small coat originally worn as men's underwear. In the middle ages, petticoats were worn by both men and women under their clothes. The petticoat became an under-skirt tied around the waist with ribbon or tapes. In the 1840s, petticoats were worn on show under an open gown. Later in the 1800s, petticoats were made of linen, cotton, **muslin** or other fine fabrics and were hidden. Warmer fabrics were worn in winter. In the 1990s, pretty petticoats again have come out on show.

Petticoats stiffened with horsebraid were called crinolines (from the French word *crin*, meaning 'horsehair'). In the 1850s, hoops made of light metal or whalebone were sewn into crinolines. Crinolines meant fewer petticoats were needed to make a fashionable shape.

▲ A crinoline of hoops and red flannel. Crinolines created the fashionable bell shape of the time.

◄ An underskirt, or petticoat, made of pink cotton with a paisley design, Australia, 1910.

So many petticoats!

In the 1840s and 1850s, a woman could wear:

- one pair of drawers (trimmed with lace)
- one flannel petticoat
- one underpetticoat, measuring two meters (6.5 feet) across
- one petticoat wadded to the knees
- one white **starched** petticoat (with **flounces**)
- two muslin petticoats
- then her dress.

Dressing Julia

Pretend Julia is a young woman living in
the 1860s, and you are helping her to dress.

1 First the camisole,
drawers and corset.

2 Then the crinoline.
This crinoline still has
the fabric. In later
crinolines, the fabric
was removed.

3 Another petticoat goes
over the crinoline.

4 The dress and sleeves are put on.

5 Then the collar, cape and hat. The outfit is complete!

CHALLENGE **1**

Answer this riddle:

Little Nancy Etticoat,
With a white petticoat,
And a red nose,
She has no feet or hands,
The longer she stands,
The shorter she stands,
The shorter she grows,
What is Nancy Etticoat?

The answer is on page 30.

Bloomers

Bloomers are any pants to the knees worn by women or girls as underwear or outerwear. Amelia Bloomer, a writer and feminist from the United States, visited England in 1851 to promote sensible clothing for women. Instead of crinolines and big long skirts, she suggested women wear a skirt to the knees and below it baggy trousers caught at the ankle. The idea of women wearing trousers, even under a skirt, was laughed at. Forty years later, when women started to ride bicycles regularly, Amelia Bloomer's outfit was worn.

► Amelia Bloomer

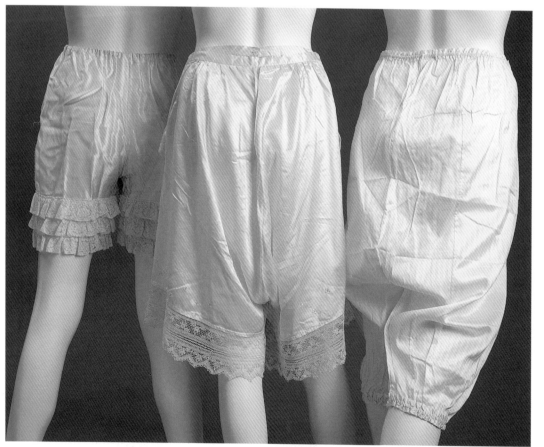

◄ These undies are called bloomers. They are all underclothes. The bloomers on the left are also called 'witches breeches'.

Negligees

Negligees and **tea gowns** were worn at home by women in the late 1800s and early 1900s. They would take off their corsets and put on a negligee after lunch. What a relief! Women would entertain their female friends at home in their tea gowns.

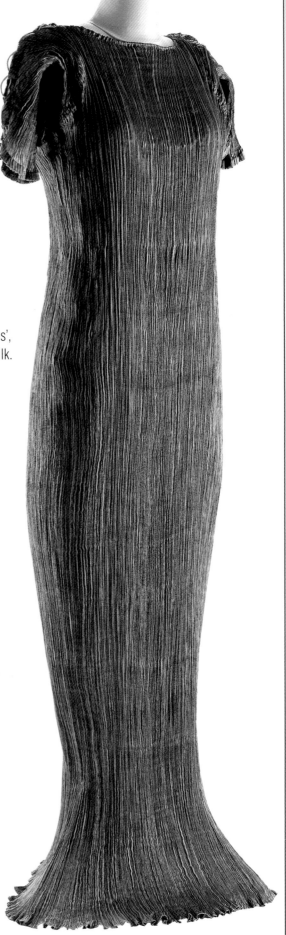

▶ This beautiful gown is an example of underwear becoming outerwear. An evening dress called 'Delphos', it is made of finely pleated, vivid green satin-weave silk. Made in Italy in 1910–20, to a design by Mariano Fortuny, the original style was called a tea gown.

CHALLENGE 2

The following underwear or fabrics are hidden in the sentences below:

- tea gown
- chemise
- cotton
- corset
- linen
- satin.

See if you can find them. Here is an example:

Suffragettes w**ho op**pose long skirts wear bloomers. ('hoop' is hidden in the sentence.)

1 You must complete a gown to finish your design course.
2 Today you can enjoy pacific or settled weather.
3 A gaberdine raincoat with a plastic hem is excellent in wet weather.
4 How many ducklings in a line? Nine!
5 The baby was put in his cot to nod off.
6 The princess sat in a bower of silk.

The answers are on page 30.

Chinese underwear

Chinese people wore starched cotton or flannelette underwear, such as loose trousers and waist-length, long-sleeved tops. A linen-like material made from **ramie** was used to make underwear. The number, quality and kind of underwear changed according to the type of work the wearer did and what they could afford.

Garments made of short lengths of fine bamboo threaded together were once worn in summer. They kept the wearer cool by stopping their outerclothes sticking to their skin. As a separate accessory, hollow bamboo stems plugged with a sticky syrup at one end were worn inside the clothes to trap fleas.

▲ The zippered pocket of these Chinese cotton underpants, made in 1994, hides money from thieves. The Chinese characters say 'High class anti-bandit underpants'.

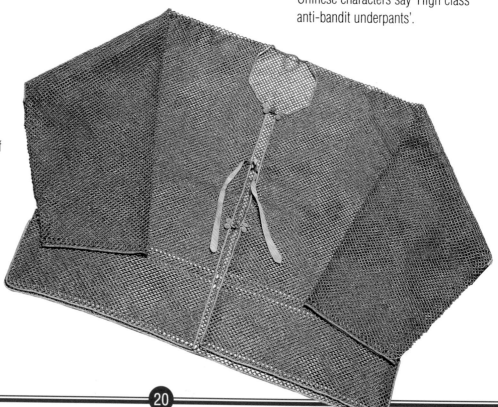

► An undervest made of woven bamboo

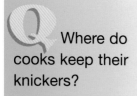
Q Where do cooks keep their knickers?

The answer is on page 30.

Embroider a singlet

Embroider your initials in chain stitch or embroider a garland of flowers around the neck of a singlet, or undershirt, in lazy-daisy stitch.

What you need:

- a singlet
- colored embroidery thread
- crewel needle
- scissors

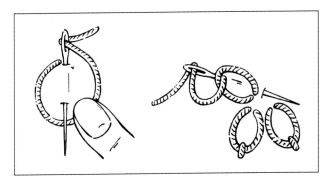

Lazy-daisy stitch

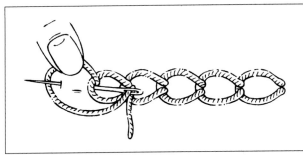

Chain stitch

Meet
Joan Lomax,
corsetiere

What is your job?

The name of my job is not used much these days. It is called a **corsetiere**. I fit underwear which adjusts the shape of the body—things like bras and panty girdles to girls, pregnant women, mothers with little babies and old women. I see women's bodies in many forms.

How long have you been a corsetiere?

For about 45 years. I applied to, and trained with, Berlei. The lessons took about two weeks, however, this was only the start of it. You need many years of experience and the right attitude to the job to do it well.

Joan Lomax

What sort of attitude?

You need 'an eye' to be able to see the body and how underwear can improve it. You also need to really care about getting every body balanced.

Tell me how you do your job.

Well, say the customer wants a new bra. I take the customer into the fitting room and ask her to take her clothes off to her underwear. I measure under the bust. We talk about whether it's a bra for everyday use or a special occasion. If it's something special, we talk about neckline and fabric. By talking to the woman and observing her, I understand her figure and its needs. I then select the right size and type of bra.

Why did you start your own business?

I was working for a big department store fitting undergarments. The stock was hidden away in cupboards and a woman had to be fitted. I was the first person to put examples of every undergarment on display. This caused a big fuss! It was because it was underwear. However, business was better, so the managers left the display. We still fitted the undergarment from the style the customer chose. Slowly this concept of personal service faded from the store. I felt I could not properly do my profession. So 20 years ago, Margaret and I started our own business.

What do you like best about your job?

Women generally don't feel good about their bodies and some have poor posture. I fit them with the correct undergarment and watch them take a big deep breath and feel proud of how they look.

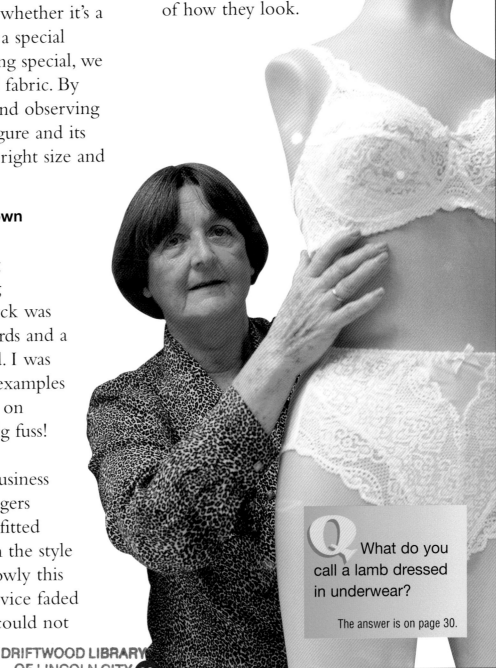

Q What do you call a lamb dressed in underwear?

The answer is on page 30.

Women's undies timeline, 1900–50

See how women's and men's underwear have changed over time. What are the big differences between men's and women's underwear?

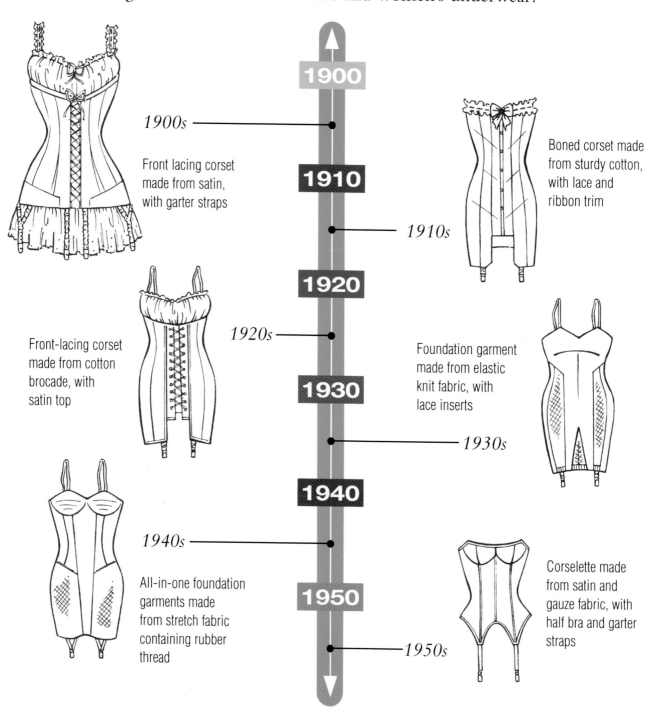

1900s
Front lacing corset made from satin, with garter straps

1910s
Boned corset made from sturdy cotton, with lace and ribbon trim

1920s
Front-lacing corset made from cotton brocade, with satin top

1930s
Foundation garment made from elastic knit fabric, with lace inserts

1940s
All-in-one foundation garments made from stretch fabric containing rubber thread

1950s
Corselette made from satin and gauze fabric, with half bra and garter straps

1900
1910
1920
1930
1940
1950

Men's undies timeline, 1900–50

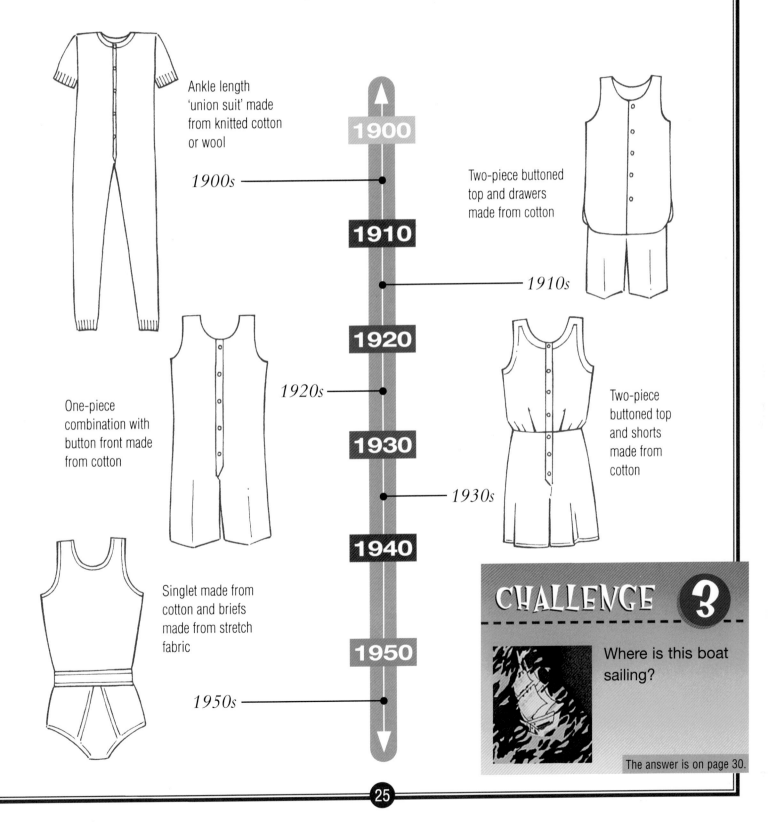

Ankle length 'union suit' made from knitted cotton or wool

1900s

1900

Two-piece buttoned top and drawers made from cotton

1910

1910s

1920

1920s

One-piece combination with button front made from cotton

1930

1930s

Two-piece buttoned top and shorts made from cotton

1940

Singlet made from cotton and briefs made from stretch fabric

1950

1950s

CHALLENGE 3

Where is this boat sailing?

The answer is on page 30.

25

Pajamas

People did not always wear special clothes to bed. About 600 years ago, people in Europe either slept in their day clothes or undressed completely. A special nightdress came into use around the 1700s—roughly the same time as the fork and handkerchief. In the 1920s, pajamas were introduced as nightwear for men and boys. Women wore pajamas to bed, but also as outerwear.

▶ Women's quilted satin slippers made by Betta, Australia, around 1985.

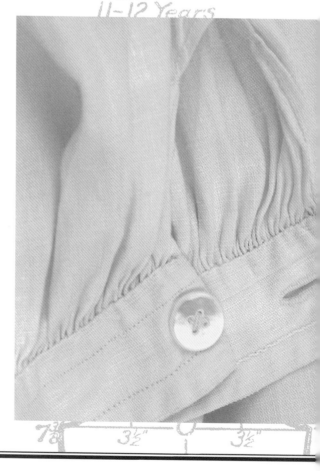

CHALLENGE 4

Find this fabric in this book.

The answer is on page 30.

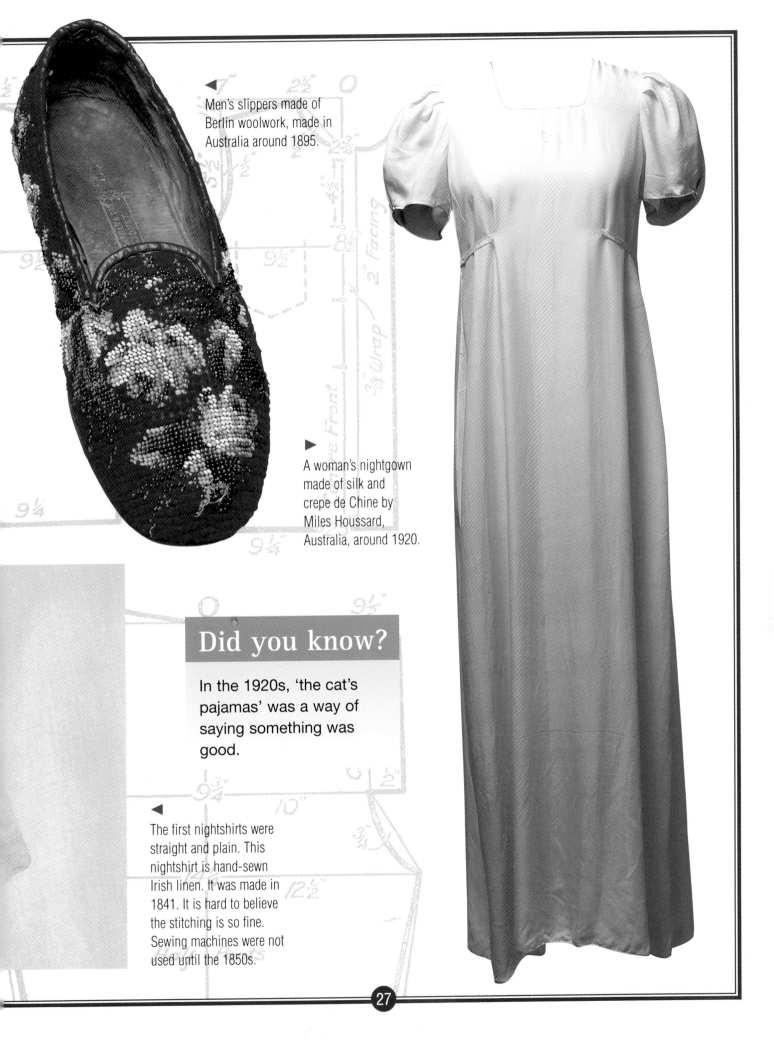

Men's slippers made of Berlin woolwork, made in Australia around 1895.

► A woman's nightgown made of silk and crepe de Chine by Miles Houssard, Australia, around 1920.

Did you know?

In the 1920s, 'the cat's pajamas' was a way of saying something was good.

◄ The first nightshirts were straight and plain. This nightshirt is hand-sewn Irish linen. It was made in 1841. It is hard to believe the stitching is so fine. Sewing machines were not used until the 1850s.

Dressing gowns

The dressing gown was a gown to put on between changes of dress or before dressing. It was a loose, long-sleeved, coat-like gown, usually made of lightweight luxurious fabric. The gown could be suitable to wear around the house and not just in the bedroom. While at times men's underwear and outerwear were very plain, their dressing gowns were very fancy. Dressing gowns are now mostly worn over nightwear.

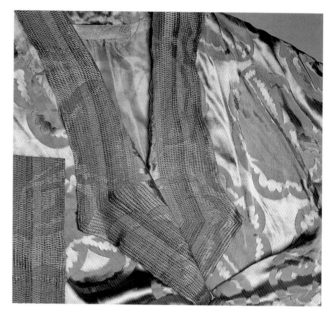

▲ A kimono wrap made of mauve synthetic material by Becker et Fils, France, 1930.

▼ A dressing gown made by Thelma White for her honeymoon, Australia, 1936.

CHALLENGE 5

Which of these three gowns is homemade? How can you tell?

The answer is on page 30.

▲ A man's dressing gown made of silk by Di Tieri, United States, around 1959.

Bedjackets and boudoir caps

Women wore **bedjackets** from around 1900. They were short, pretty jackets to wear over a nightgown while sitting up in bed. **Boudoir caps**, or nightcaps, were worn much earlier. From the 1500s, men wore nightcaps. In 1557, a doctor advised that nightcaps should be red, while in 1602 another doctor said: 'Let your night cappe have a hole in the top through which the vapour may go out.'

▶ A lady's bedjacket made of cream net lace and lined with pink silk.

▼ Fine cream cap, hand embroidered and lace trimmed, made around 1805.

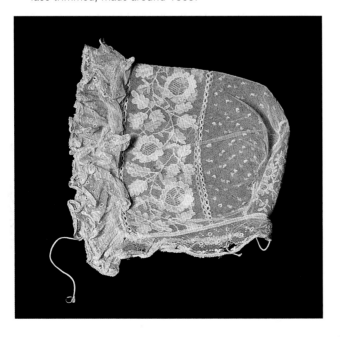

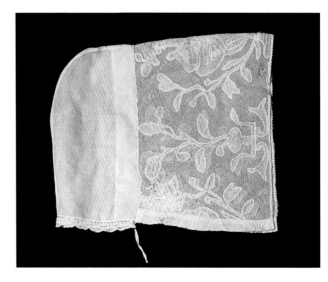

▲ White linen woman's cap, with border of bobbin lace, made in the early 1900s in Holland.

The changing shape of underwear

The body shape changes according to where and when you live. Body shapes can be changed by what we wear underneath our clothes. Underwear also decorates and protects our bodies.

Underclothes are private clothes. But as we have seen, they can travel—from being hidden to being on show. Underwear changes form and style according to the desired body shape of the decade, year or moment.

This petticoat worn beneath an open robe, made in England in 1760, helped make the female body look as though it had very wide hips.

Answers

Page 9
They are sleeves that can easily be removed to wash.

Page 17
Nancy Etticoat is a candle.

Page 19
1 You must comple**te a gown** to finish your design course. (tea gown)

2 Today you can enjoy pacifi**c or set**tled weather. (corset)

3 A gabadine raincoat with a plasti**c hem is e**xcellent in wet weather. (chemise)

4 How many ducklings in a **line**? **N**ine! (linen)

5 The baby was put in his **cot to n**od off. (cotton)

6 The princess **sat in** a bower of silk. (satin)

Page 20
In the pantry (pant-ry).

Page 23
Bra Bra Black Sheep.

Page 25
The boat is on the man's dressing gown on page 28.

Page 26
The fabric is from the bedjacket on page 29.

Page 28
The dressing gown without the label on the neck is homemade. Thelma White made it for her honeymoon in 1936.

Glossary

bedjackets	short, pretty jackets worn over a nightgown while sitting up in bed
bloomers	pants that come down to the knee, worn by women as underwear or outerwear
bodice	a part of a woman's dress, above the waist
boudoir caps	head coverings worn to bed
bustles	underwear made of padding, horsehair or whalebone to push out a dress to give the appearance of a big bottom
camisole	a type of singlet, or undershirt
chemise	a sleeveless, knee-length shirt
corsetiere	a person who fits people for underwear
corsets	stiff garments worn around the torso and mostly used to make a smaller waist or raise the breasts. Worn by men and women
crinoline	a cage-like structure of hoops to push a skirt out. The diameter of the hoops increases from top to bottom, giving a cone shape
drawers	underwear covering the bottom half of the body and legs. Not commonly worn until the 1900s
flannel	a soft woollen fabric available in a range of textures and thicknesses
flounces	ruffles or frills made of fabric
linen	fabric made from the flax plant. Made originally in India and China 5,000 years ago
muslin	a plain woven cotton
negligees	informal coats worn at home in the evenings only in front of friends and family (pronounced 'neg-li-jays')
panniers	hoops covered in fabric and tied to a woman's waist to give her the appearance of very wide hips and legs
piping	a very narrow cord used as a decorative edging on some clothes
ramie	a plant from which a strong glossy fiber can be spun and woven into fabric
starched	to have stiffened a fabric by applying an odorless, tasteless powdery substance obtained from plants and diluted with water
tea gowns	pretty coats or dresses worn without a corset

Index

Photo credits

All objects featured in this publication are from the Powerhouse Museum collection, unless otherwise indicated. The Museum acknowledges the many generous donations of objects, which form a significant part of its collection.
★ Indicates photographs of museum objects reproduced with the permission of the designer or maker. Photographs are by the Powerhouse Museum unless otherwise indicated.

Page 4 Funkessentials poster★ by Sara Thorn and Bruce Slorach; page 12 Ada Lovelace, photo courtesy The British Museum; pages 22/23 Joan Lomax; pages 24/25 Timelines based on information from Turner Wilcox, R, *The Dictionary of Costume*, BT Batsford, London, 1992.

Please visit the Powerhouse Museum at **www.phm.gov.au**